I love reading

Dinosaur Battles
by Monica Hughes

Consultant: Dougal Dixon

tickto

Copyright © **ticktock Entertainment Ltd 2007**
First published in Great Britain in 2007 by **ticktock Media Ltd.,**
Unit 2, Orchard Business Centre, North Farm Road, Tunbridge Wells, Kent TN2 3XF

We would like to thank: Shirley Bickler and Suzanne Baker

ISBN 978 1 84696 608 8 pbk
Printed in China

Picture credits
t=top, b=bottom, c=centre, l-left, r=right, OFC= outside front cover
Lisa Alderson: 13, 16-17, 22tl; John Alston: 7t, 6b, 8b; Simon Mendez: 17tr, 19, 23tr;
Natural History Museum: 12, 21; Luis Rey: 1, 4, 5, 10-11, 15, 18, 20, 22br, 23r, 23c;
Science Photo Library: 9; Shutterstock: 7b.

Every effort has been made to trace the copyright holders, and we apologise in advance for any
unintentional omissions. We would be pleased to insert the appropriate acknowledgements in any
subsequent edition of this publication.

CONTENTS

Fighting dinosaurs

Some dinosaurs did a lot of fighting.

Some dinosaurs hit
each another with their
hard heads.

This dinosaur hit out with its big claws.

Segnosaurus
seg-no-sor-us

Dinosaurs that liked to eat meat

Meat-eating dinosaurs ate other dinosaurs.

Dilophosaurus was a small dinosaur that ate meat. It ran very fast to catch its food.

**Dilophosaurus
dil-o-fo-sor-us**

T. rex had a huge mouth and lots of teeth.
A whole cow could fit in its mouth.

Tyrannosaurus rex
tie-ran-o-sor-us rex

Allosaurus

Allosaurus was one of the biggest meat-eating dinosaurs.

It was big and strong and good at fighting.

It had big claws and about 70 big teeth.

It killed big plant-eating dinosaurs.

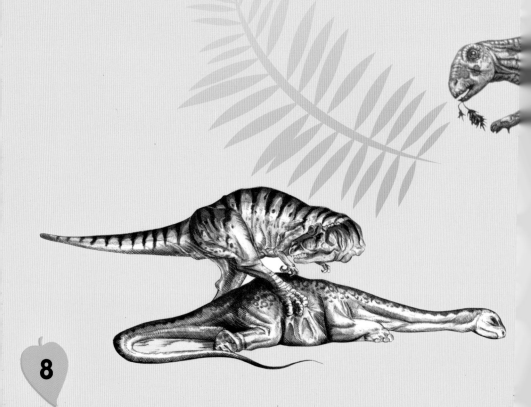

Allosaurus
al-o-sor-us

9

Small killer dinosaurs

Not all the meat-eating
dinosaurs were big.

Deinonychus
die-non-ee-cus

Some small
dinosaurs hunted
together.

This made it easy
for them to kill a
big dinosaur.

Dinosaurs that liked to eat plants

Some were very tall and some were very long. Some were both!

The tall ones reached up to the tops of trees.

Seismosaurus
size-mo-sor-us

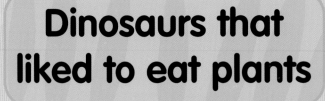

Many plant-eating dinosaurs were too big for meat-eaters to attack.

Sauroposeidon
saw-ro-po-si-don

Heterodontosaurus

This plant-eating dinosaur ran very fast.

It also looked very scary.

So some meat-eating dinosaurs ran away from it.

It was saved from being eaten!

Heterodontosaurus
het-er-o-don-to-saw-rus

Horns and spikes

Some plant-eating dinosaurs had to fight meat-eating dinosaurs.

They had horns or spikes to stop the meat-eating dinosaurs killing them.

Sauropelta
sor-o-pel-ta

Triceratops was a dinosaur
with three horns on its head.

Triceratops
try-serra-tops

Spikes

Sauropelta had
spikes on its neck.

Plates

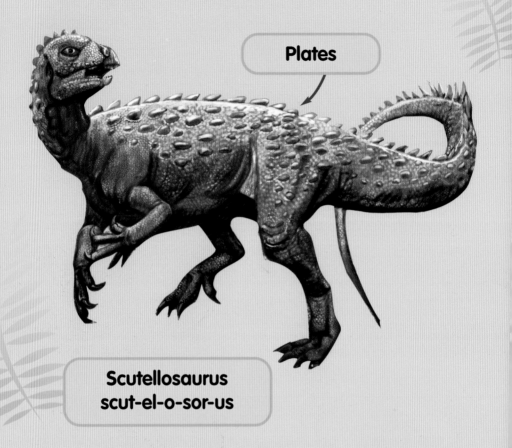

Plates

Scutellosaurus
scut-el-o-sor-us

Some plant-eating dinosaurs had plates on their backs to protect them in a fight.

This dinosaur had small plates on its back and tail.

This dinosaur had two rows of plates on its back and tail.

Plates

Stegosaurus
steg-o-sor-us

Armour and clubs

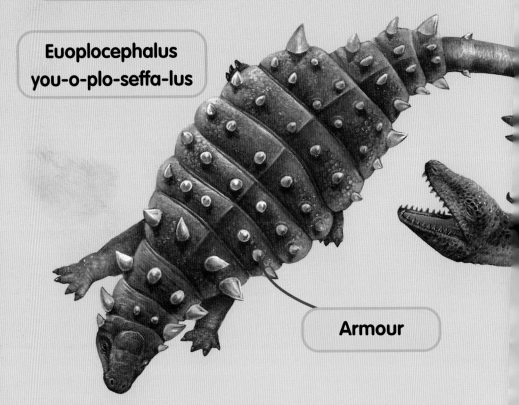

Euoplocephalus
you-o-plo-seffa-lus

Armour

Some plant-eating dinosaurs had armour.

Some dinosaurs had a tail with
a club on the end.

They could hit a meat-eating
dinosaur with the club.

Club

Tarchia
tar-kee-a

This dinosaur had armour
and a tail club, too.

21

Thinking and talking about dinosaurs

Which dinosaur had two rows of plates on its back and tail?

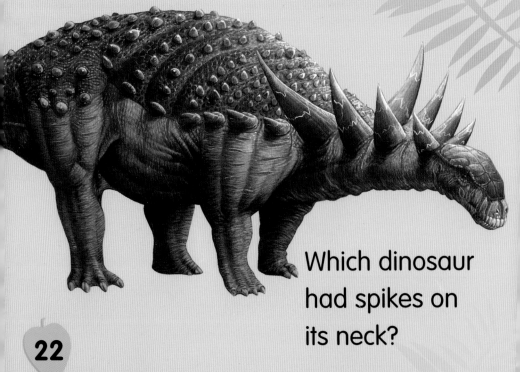

Which dinosaur had spikes on its neck?

What did
Euoplocephalus do
with its tail club?

Was this
dinosaur a
plant-eater or
a meat-eater?

Which dinosaur
had big claws?

23

Activities

What did you think of this book?

 Brilliant **Good** **OK**

• • • • • • • • • • • • • •

Which one of these ate plants?

Allosaurus • Stegosaurus • Tyrannosaurus Rex

• • • • • • • • • • • • •

Invent a dinosaur! Draw a big picture and label it. Use these words.

spikes • club tail • plates
horns • armour

• • • • • • • • • • • • •

Who is the author of this book?
Have you read *Dinosaur Giants*
by the same author?